A DOZEN A DAY COUNTING RHYTHM

Rhythm Exercises for

ALL INSTRUMENTS

To access audio, visit:
www.halleonard.com/mylibrary

Enter Code
4249-2762-2693-6725

ISBN 979-8-3501-6365-0

Exclusively Distributed By

Visit Hal Leonard Online at
www.halleonard.com

World headquarters, contact:
Hal Leonard
7777 West Bluemound Road
Milwaukee, WI 53213
Email: info@halleonard.com

In Europe, contact:
Hal Leonard Europe Limited
Dettingen Way
Bury St Edmunds, Suffolk, IP33 3YB
Email: info@halleonardeurope.com

In Australia, contact:
Hal Leonard Australia Pty. Ltd.
4 Lentara Court
Cheltenham, Victoria, 3192 Australia
Email: info@halleonard.com.au

A DOZEN A DAY

Edna-Mae Burnam's *A Dozen a Day* books have been enjoyed by millions of piano students around the world since they were first published in 1954.

This addition to the series is intended for learners of any instrument, addressing the challenge of counting and understanding rhythm at beginner level. It is a practical handbook presenting sequenced, unpitched exercises, each preceded by a counting example for comprehension. A rhythmic index can be found on page 33. Here, rhythmic values and exercises are listed in order of appearance, for ease of reference.

Rhythmic values and metres are aligned with the first four books in Edna-Mae Burnam's piano series. The following concepts are covered:

- Counting Method
- Beat and Beat Subdivision
- Note Values and Rests:
  i. Whole Note
  ii. Half Note
  iii. Quarter Note
  iv. Eighth Note
  v. 16th Note
- Ties and Dotted Notes
- Simple Time Signatures
- Compound Time Signatures

Exercises in this book are accompanied by play-along audio. The audio tracks also include several metronome clicks—beats at different speeds for rigorous, personal practice. Where the examples have four beats per measure (e.g., 4/4 or 12/8), there is one measure of clicks. For all other time signatures, there are two whole measures of clicks. The exercises all carry a metronome marking. Practicing different tempos will aid a better understanding of rhythmic groups and the relationship between various note symbols. To access the accompanying audio, simply look for the icon, go to www.halleonard.com/mylibrary, and enter the code found on page 1 of this book. This will grant you instant access to every file. You can download to your computer, tablet, or phone, or stream the audio live.

COUNTING RHYTHM

A DOZEN A DAY

CONTENTS

GROUP I 4

COUNTING TIME 4
1. Steady Walk on the Spot 4
2. Morning Stretches 5
3. Step and Stride 5
4. Walk and Rest for Four 5
5. Big Strides 6
6. On Your Toes 6

COUNTING TIME 6
7. Beginner Tightrope 7
8. Catch Your Breath 7
9. Sit Up, Then Lie Down 7
10. Tough Chin-Ups 8
11. Tapping the Hammer 8
12. Right on Time and Ready to Go 8

GROUP II 9

COUNTING TIME 9
1. Bouncing the Ball 9
2. Boxing 10
3. Playground Jump-Rope Chant 10
4. High-Knees Marching 10
5. Power Walk 11
6. Little Steps 11

COUNTING TIME 11
7. Baton Rhythm 12
8. Punchbag Exercise 12
9. Hammering Nails 12
10. Running in the Dark 13
11. Time Out 13
12. Right on Time and Ready to Go 13

GROUP III 14

COUNTING TIME 14
1. Waltzing on Stilts 15
2. Tiptoe, Don't Get Caught 15
3. A Bit Stop-Start 15
4. March on the Spot 16
5. Stepping in Time 16
6. Baby Steps 16

COUNTING TIME 17
7. Brushing Teeth 18
8. Working the Punchbag 18
9. Breakdance 18
10. Disco Time 19
11. Gentle Skip 19
12. Right on Time and Ready to Go 19

GROUP IV 20

COUNTING TIME 20
1. Tied Together for a Mountain Walk 21
2. Walking Dotty 21
3. Stretch It Out 21
4. One Step Ahead 22
5. Lifting Weights 22
6. Awkward Dancing 22

COUNTING TIME 23
7. 1-and-a, 2-and-Away We Go! 24
8. Wriggling Toes 24
9. Twirling on Toes 24
10. Graceful Swinging 25
11. A Hop and a Skip 25
12. Right on Time and Ready to Go 25

GROUP V 26

COUNTING TIME 26
1. Triplet Squats 27
2. Groovy Dance 27
3. Wobbly Piggyback 27
4. Gym Beats 28
5. Street Dance 28
6. At a Canter 28

COUNTING TIME 29
7. Stumble, Trip 30
8. Tiptoes 30
9. On the Water 30
10. Keepie-Uppies 31
11. Down the Rope, Inch by Inch 31
12. Right on Time and Ready to Go 31

GROUP RHYTHM SUMMARY 32

RHYTHM INDEX 33

Group I

COUNTING TIME

1. Steady Walk on the Spot

2. Morning Stretches

♩ = 120

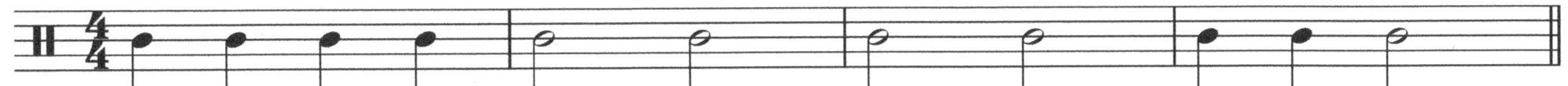

3. Step and Stride

♩ = 80

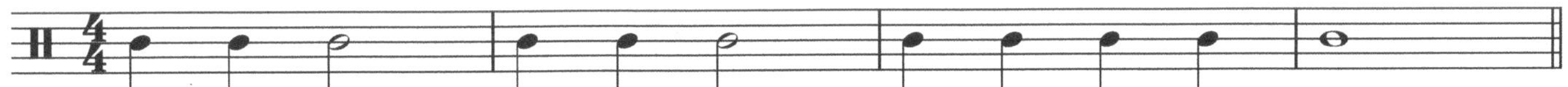

4. Walk and Rest for Four

♩ = 100

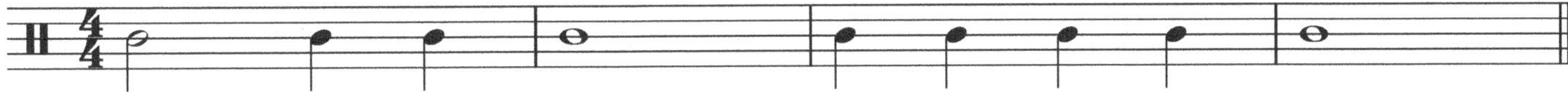

5. Big Strides

6. On Your Toes

COUNTING TIME

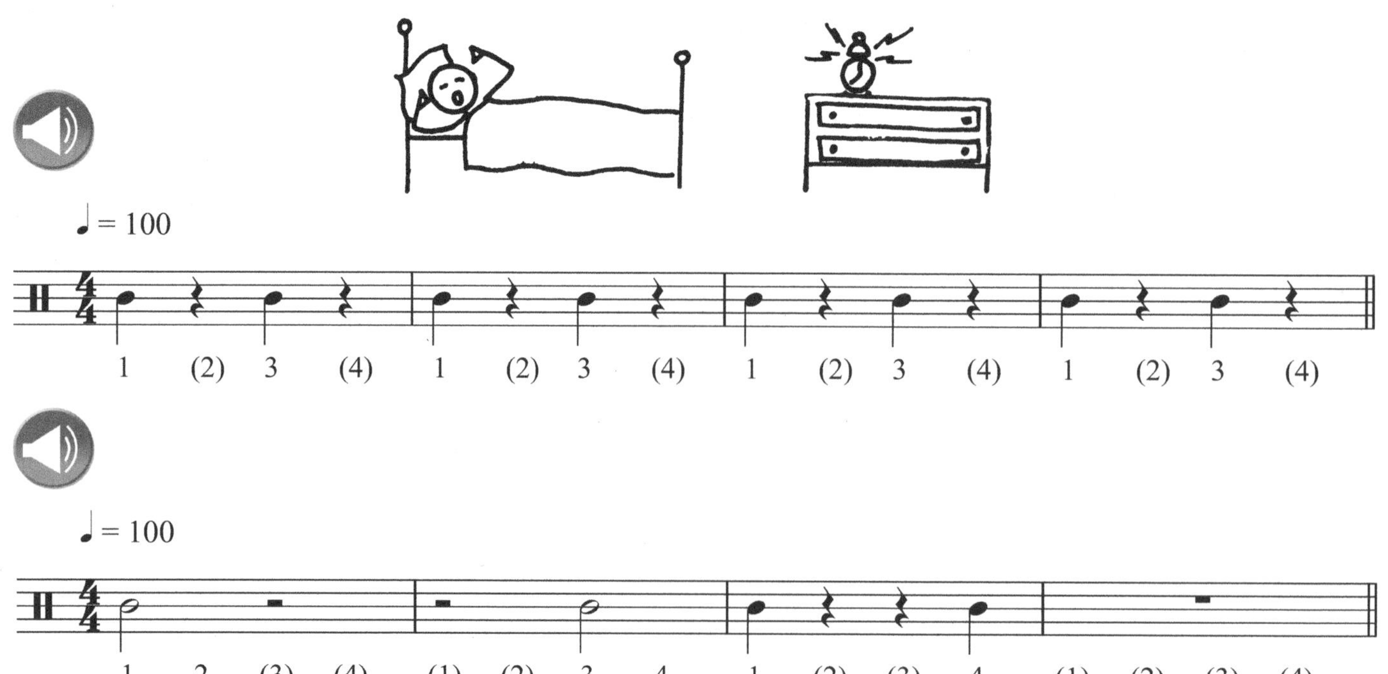

7. Beginner Tightrope

8. Catch Your Breath

9. Sit Up, Then Lie Down

10. Tough Chin-Ups

11. Tapping the Hammer

12. Right on Time and Ready to Go

Group II

COUNTING TIME

1. Bouncing the Ball

2. Boxing

3. Playground Jump-Rope Chant

4. High-Knees Marching

5. Power Walk

♩ = 100

6. Little Steps

♩ = 60

COUNTING TIME

♩ = 60

7. Baton Rhythm

♩ = 100

8. Punchbag Exercise

♩ = 80

9. Hammering Nails

♩ = 60

10. Running in the Dark

11. Time Out

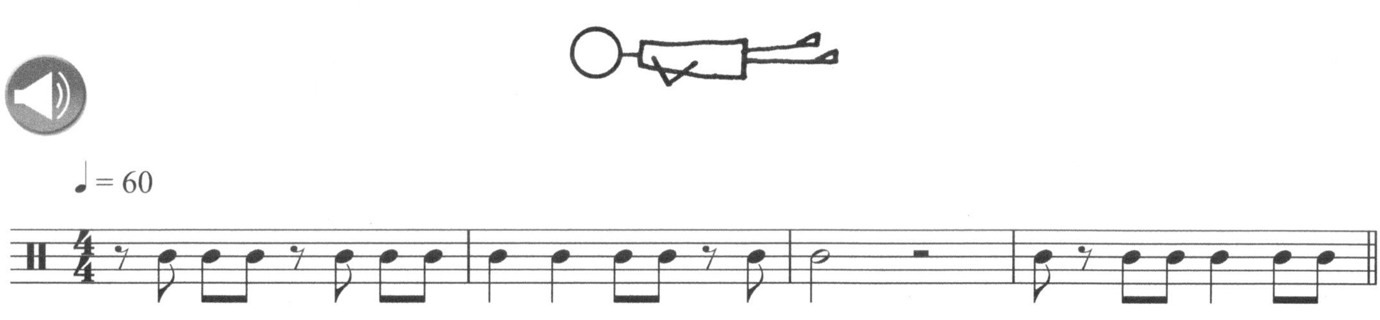

12. Right on Time and Ready to Go

♩ = 110

Group III

COUNTING TIME

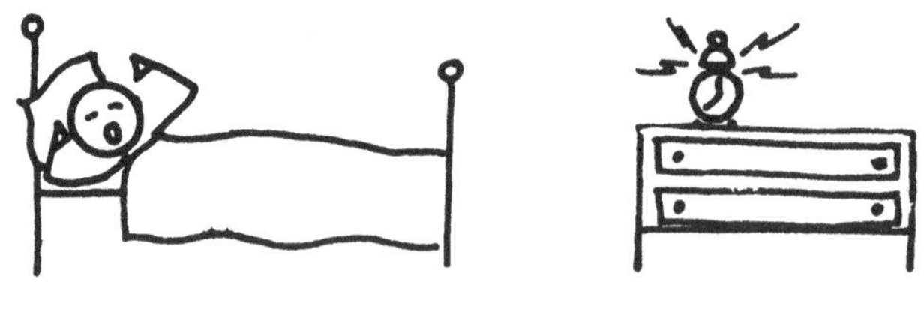

1 2 3 1 2 3

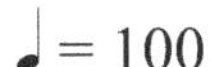

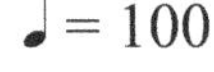

1. Waltzing on Stilts

♩ = 60

2. Tiptoe, Don't Get Caught

♩ = 90

3. A Bit Stop-Start

♩ = 110

4. March on the Spot

5. Stepping in Time

6. Baby Steps

COUNTING TIME

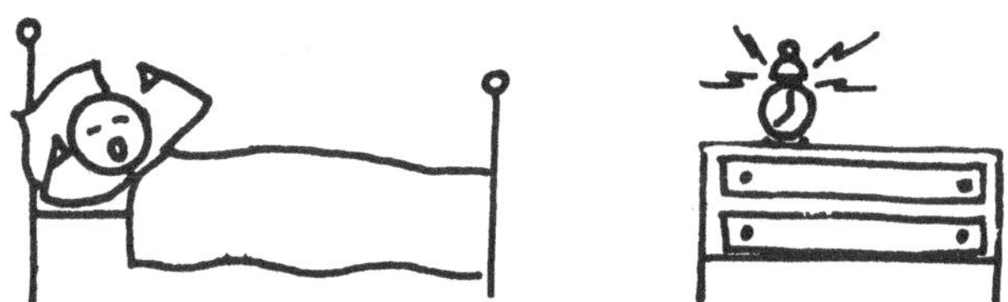

♩ = 50

7. Brushing Teeth

8. Working the Punchbag

9. Breakdance

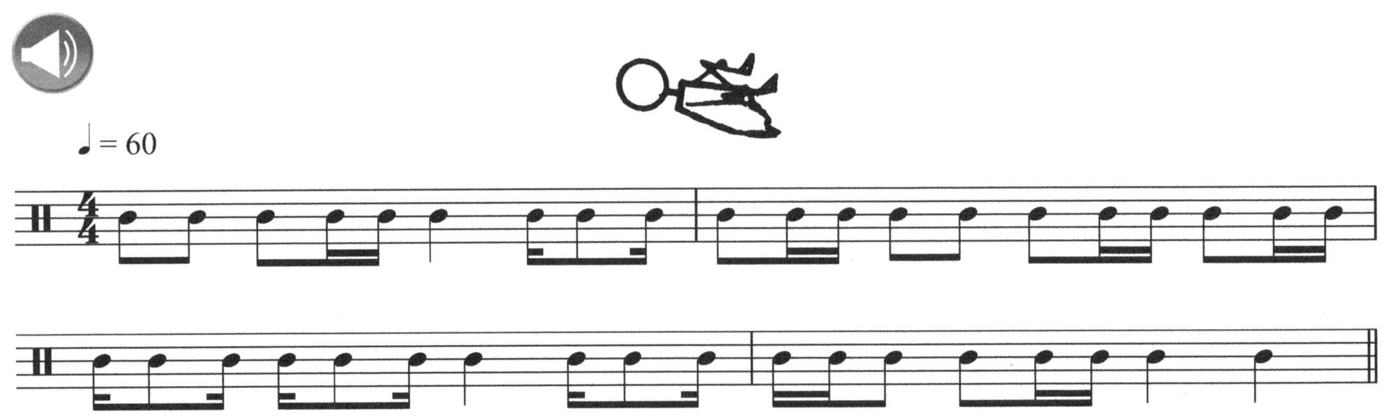

10. Disco Time

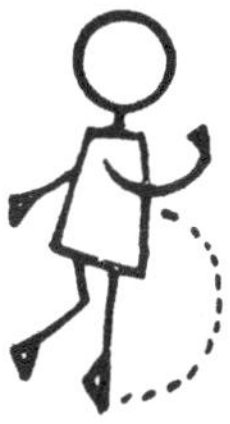

♩ = 80

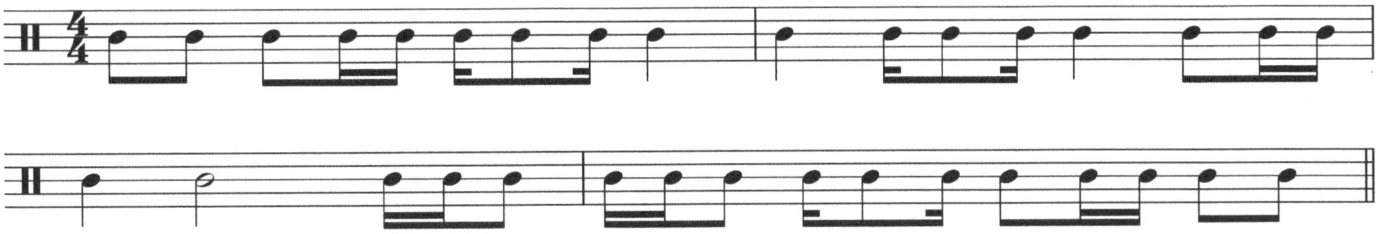

11. Gentle Skip

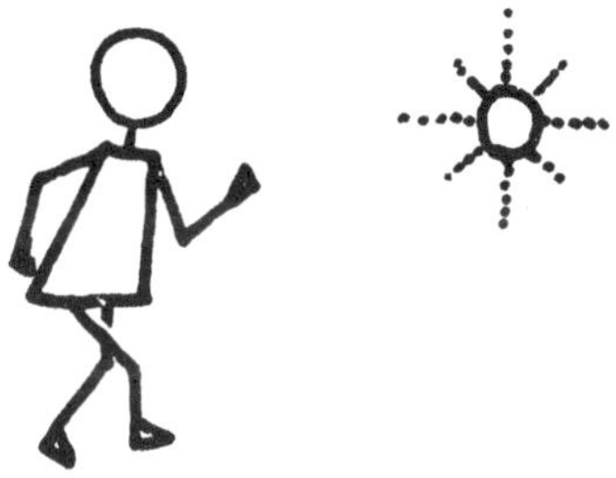

♩ = 40

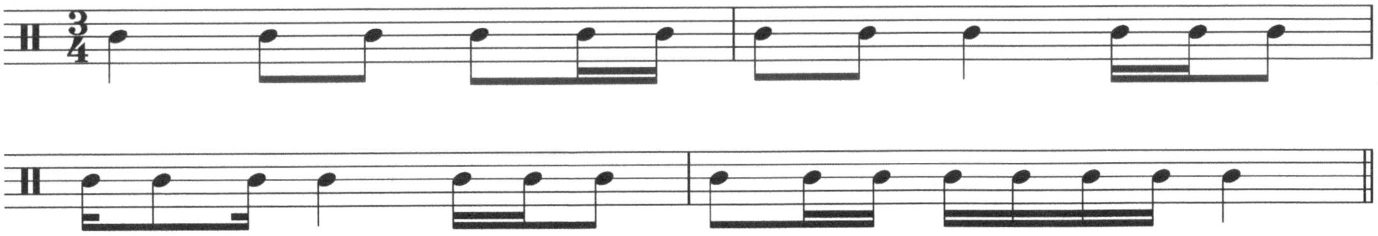

12. Right on Time and Ready to Go

♩ = 60

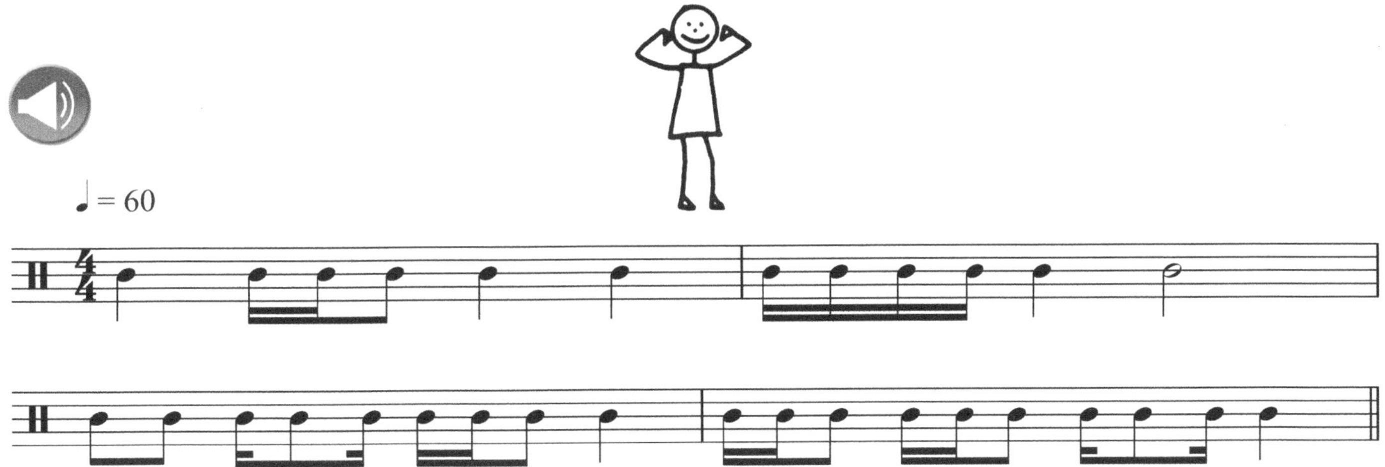

Group IV

COUNTING TIME

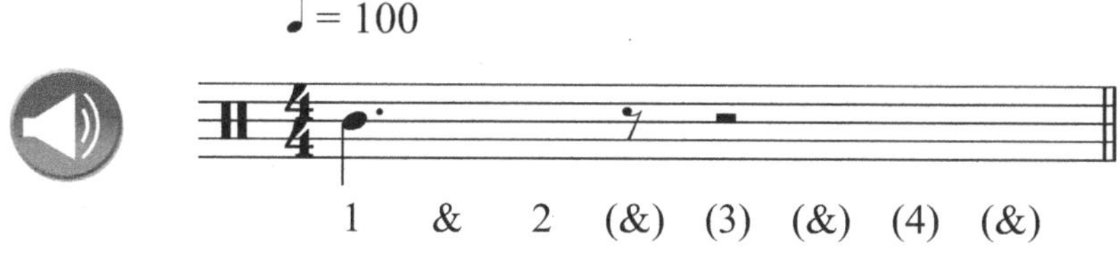

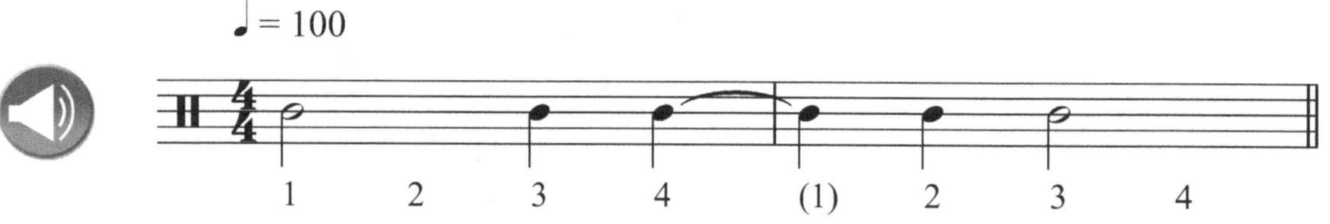

1. Tied Together for a Mountain Walk

2. Walking Dotty

♩ = 90

3. Stretch It Out

4. One Step Ahead

5. Lifting Weights

6. Awkward Dancing

COUNTING TIME

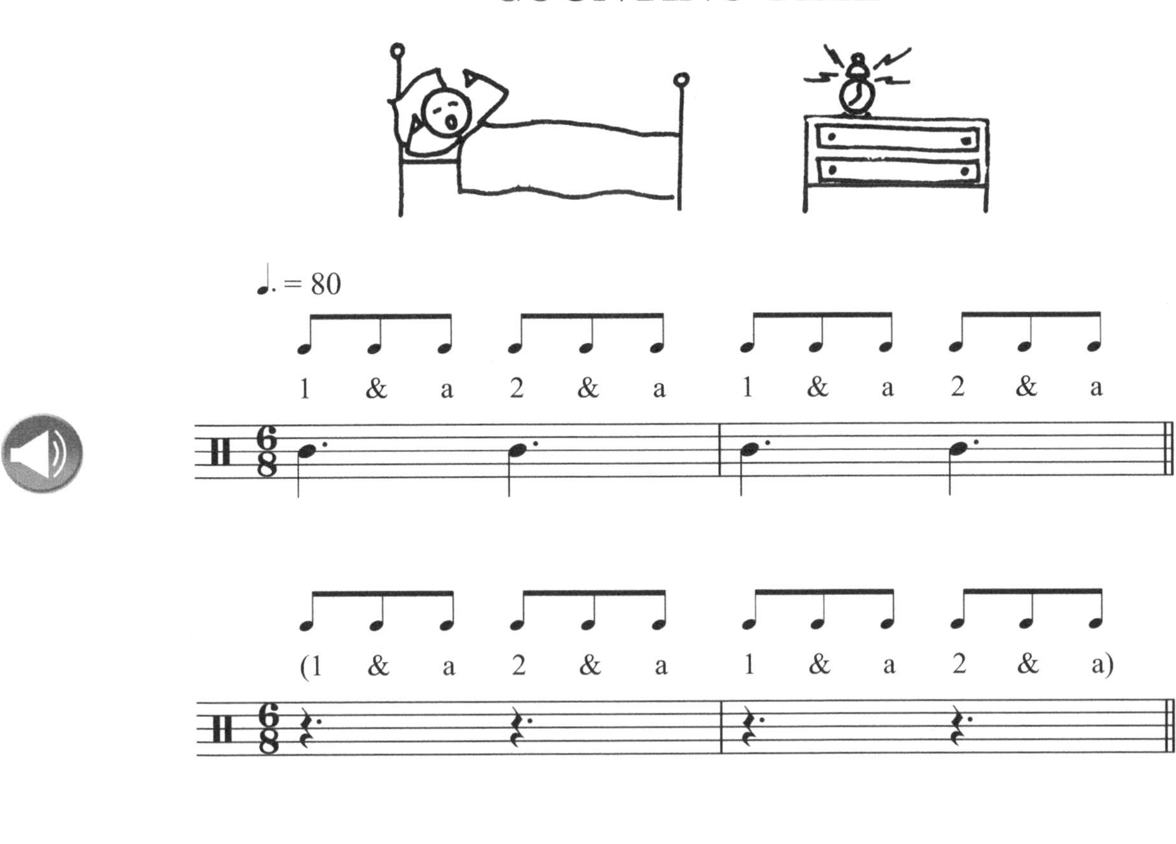

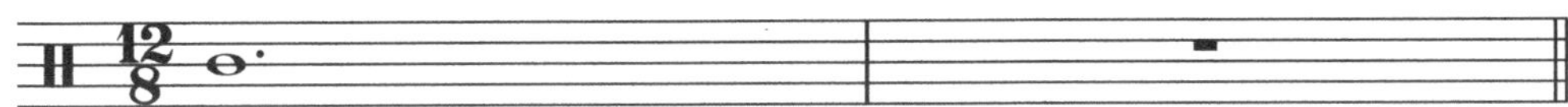

7. 1-and-a, 2-and-Away We Go!

8. Wriggling Toes

9. Twirling on Toes

10. Graceful Swinging

♩. = 50

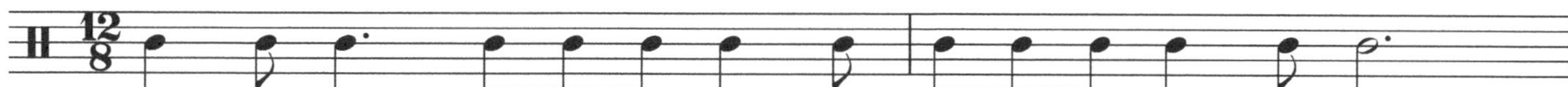

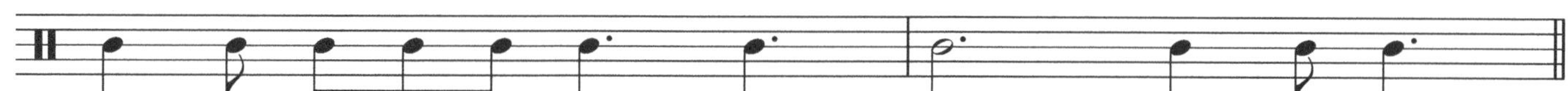

11. A Hop and a Skip

♩. = 60

12. Right on Time and Ready to Go

♩. = 70

Group V

COUNTING TIME

1. Triplet Squats

2. Groovy Dance

3. Wobbly Piggyback

4. Gym Beats

5. Street Dance

6. At a Canter

COUNTING TIME

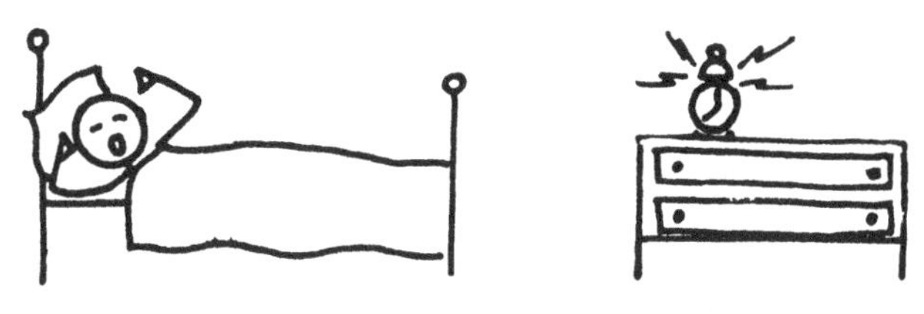

♩ = 60

♩ = 30 / ♩ = 70

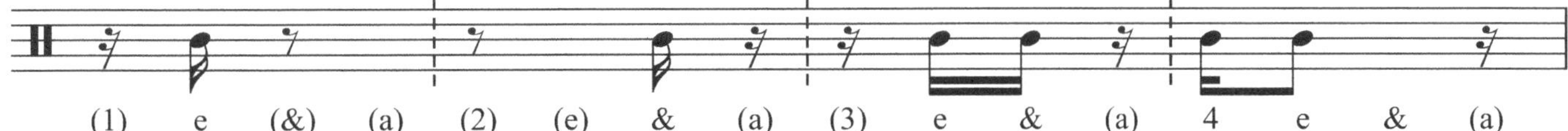

7. Stumble, Trip

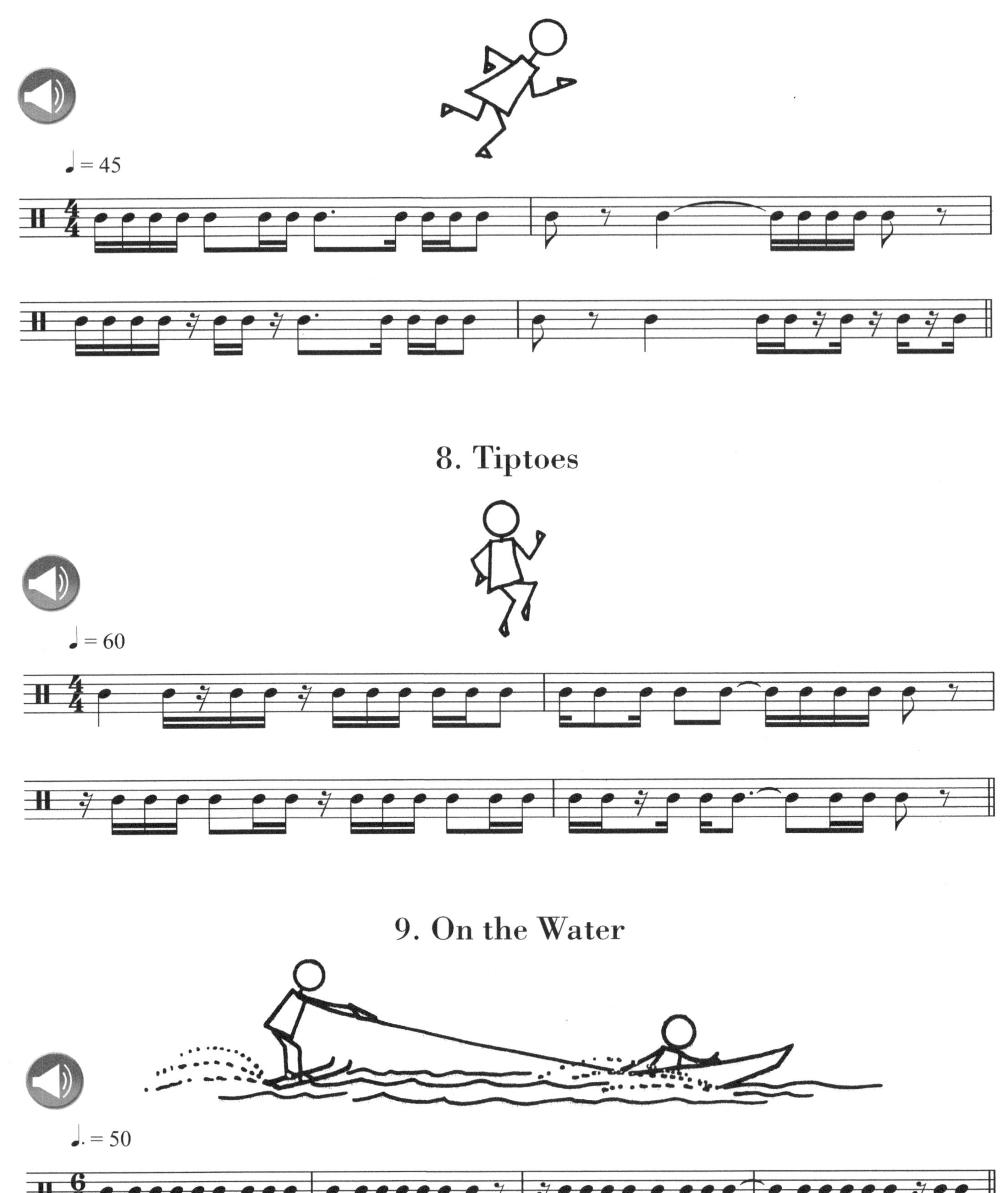

8. Tiptoes

9. On the Water

10. Keepie-Uppies

11. Down the Rope, Inch by Inch

12. Right on Time and Ready to Go

GROUP RHYTHM SUMMARY

GROUP I

Whole Note Value and Rest

Half Note Value and Rest

Quarter Note Value and Rest

Simple Quadruple Meter

GROUP II

Group I Note Values and Rests

Eighth Note Value (in Pairs and in Fours)

Single Eighth Note Value and Rest

GROUP III

Groups I and II Note Values and Rests

Simple Duple Meter

Simple Triple Meter

16th Note Value (in Fours and Beamed with Eighth Note)

GROUP IV

Groups I, II, and III Note Values and Rests

Dotted-Quarter Note Value and Rest

Dotted-Half Note Value

Beamed Dotted-Eighth–16th Note Values

Tied Notes

Compound Meters

GROUP V

Groups I, II, III, and IV Note Values and Rests

Triplet Eighth-Note Groupings

Triplet Quarter-Note Groupings

Single 16th-Note Rest

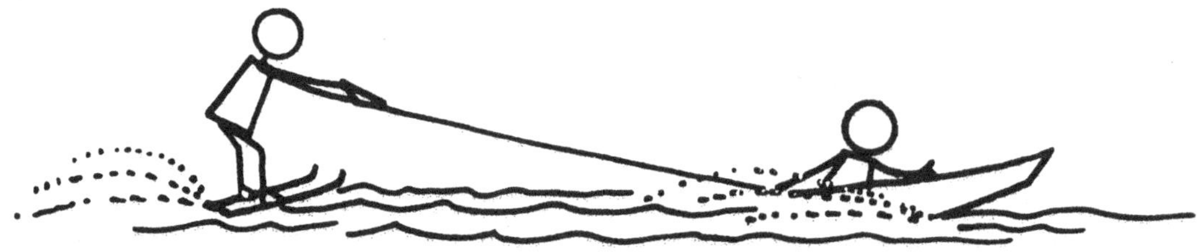

RHYTHM INDEX

QUARTER NOTE

TITLE	Grp.	No.	Page
Steady Walk on the Spot	I	1	4
Morning Stretches	I	2	5
Step and Stride	I	3	5
Walk and Rest for Four	I	4	5
Big Strides	I	5	6
On Your Toes	I	6	6
Beginner Tightrope	I	7	7
Catch Your Breath	I	8	7
Sit Up, Then Lie Down	I	9	7
Tough Chin-Ups	I	10	8
Tapping the Hammer	I	11	8
Right on Time and Ready to Go	I	12	8
Bouncing the Ball	II	1	9
Boxing	II	2	10
Playground Jump-Rope Chant	II	3	10
High-Knees Marching	II	4	10
Power Walk	II	5	11
Little Steps	II	6	11
Baton Rhythm	II	7	12
Punchbag Exercise	II	8	12
Hammering Nails	II	9	12
Running in the Dark	II	10	13
Time Out	II	11	13
Right on Time and Ready to Go	II	12	13
Waltzing on Stilts	III	1	15
Tiptoe, Don't Get Caught	III	2	15
A Bit Stop-Start	III	3	15
March on the Spot	III	4	16
Stepping in Time	III	5	16
Baby Steps	III	6	16
Brushing Teeth	III	7	18
Working the Punchbag	III	8	18
Breakdance	III	9	18
Disco Time	III	10	19
Gentle Skip	III	11	19
Right on Time and Ready to Go	III	12	19
Tied Together for a Mountain Walk	IV	1	21
Walking Dotty	IV	2	21
Stretch It Out	IV	3	21
One Step Ahead	IV	4	22
Lifting Weights	IV	5	22
Awkward Dancing	IV	6	22
1-and-a, 2-and-Away We Go!	IV	7	24
Wriggling Toes	IV	8	24
Twirling on Toes	IV	9	24
Graceful Swinging	IV	10	25
Right on Time and Ready to Go	IV	12	25
Triplet Squats	V	1	27
Groovy Dance	V	2	27
Wobbly Piggyback	V	3	27
Gym Beats	V	4	28
Street Dance	V	5	28
At a Canter	V	6	28
Stumble, Trip	V	7	30
Tiptoes	V	8	30
Keepie-Uppies	V	10	31

HALF NOTE

TITLE	Grp.	No.	Page
Steady Walk on the Spot	I	1	4
Morning Stretches	I	2	5
Step and Stride	I	3	5
Walk and Rest for Four	I	4	5
Big Strides	I	5	6
On Your Toes	I	6	6
Beginner Tightrope	I	7	7
Catch Your Breath	I	8	7
Sit Up, Then Lie Down	I	9	7
Tough Chin-Ups	I	10	8
Tapping the Hammer	I	11	8
Right on Time and Ready to Go	I	12	8
Boxing	II	2	10
Playground Jump-Rope Chant	II	3	10
High-Knees Marching	II	4	10
Little Steps	II	6	11
Punchbag Exercise	II	8	12

WHOLE NOTE

QUARTER REST

HALF REST

WHOLE REST/ WHOLE MEASURE REST

PAIRED EIGHTH NOTES

EIGHTH NOTES (IN FOURS)

EIGHTH REST

SINGLE EIGHTH NOTE

TITLE	*Grp.*	*No.*	*Page*
Wriggling Toes	IV	8	24
Twirling on Toes	IV	9	24
Graceful Swinging	IV	10	25
A Hop and a Skip	IV	11	25
Right on Time and Ready to Go	IV	12	25
Groovy Dance	V	2	27
Wobbly Piggyback	V	3	27
Gym Beats	V	4	28
Street Dance	V	5	28
At a Canter	V	6	28
Stumble, Trip	V	7	30
Tiptoes	V	8	30
On the Water	V	9	30
Down the Rope, Inch by Inch	V	11	31

16TH NOTES (IN FOURS)

TITLE	*Grp.*	*No.*	*Page*
Brushing Teeth	III	7	18
Working the Punchbag	III	8	18
Gentle Skip	III	11	19
Right on Time and Ready to Go	III	12	19
Stumble, Trip	V	7	30
Tiptoes	V	8	30

EIGHTH NOTE BEAMED WITH TWO 16TH NOTES

TITLE	*Grp.*	*No.*	*Page*
Brushing Teeth	III	7	18
Working the Punchbag	III	8	18
Breakdance	III	9	18
Disco Time	III	10	19
Gentle Skip	III	11	19
Right on Time and Ready to Go	III	12	19
Walking Dotty	IV	2	21
Stretch It Out	IV	3	21
One Step Ahead	IV	4	22
Lifting Weights	IV	5	22
A Hop and a Skip	IV	11	25
Street Dance	V	5	28
Stumble, Trip	V	7	30
Tiptoes	V	8	30
Keepie-Uppies	V	10	31
Right on Time and Ready to Go	V	12	31

EIGHTH NOTES AND 16TH NOTES IN COMPOUND BEAMING

TITLE	*Grp.*	*No.*	*Page*
1-and-a, 2-and-Away We Go!	IV	7	24
Wriggling Toes	IV	8	24
Twirling on Toes	IV	9	24
A Hop and a Skip	IV	11	25
On the Water	V	9	30
Down the Rope, Inch by Inch	V	11	31

DOTTED-QUARTER NOTE

TITLE	*Grp.*	*No.*	*Page*
Walking Dotty	IV	2	21
Stretch It Out	IV	3	21
One Step Ahead	IV	4	22
Lifting Weights	IV	5	22
1-and-a, 2-and-Away We Go!	IV	7	24
Wriggling Toes	IV	8	24
Twirling on Toes	IV	9	24
Graceful Swinging	IV	10	25
A Hop and a Skip	IV	11	25
Right on Time and Ready to Go	IV	12	25
Street Dance	V	5	28

DOTTED-HALF NOTE

TITLE	*Grp.*	*No.*	*Page*
Tied Together for a Mountain Walk	IV	1	21
Walking Dotty	IV	2	21
Lifting Weights	IV	5	22
Graceful Swinging	IV	10	25
Right on Time and Ready to Go	IV	12	25

DOTTED-EIGHTH NOTE BEAMED WITH 16TH NOTE

TITLE	*Grp.*	*No.*	*Page*
Walking Dotty	IV	2	21
1-and-a, 2-and-Away We Go!	IV	7	24

DOTTED-QUARTER REST

EIGHTH NOTES (IN THREES)

TIED NOTES

TRIPLET EIGHTH NOTES

TRIPLET QUARTER NOTES

16TH REST

SIMPLE QUADRUPLE METER

TITLE	*Grp.*	*No.*	*Page*
Hammering Nails	II	9	12
Running in the Dark	II	10	13
Time Out	II	11	13
Right on Time and Ready to Go	II	12	13
Brushing Teeth	III	7	18
Breakdance	III	9	18
Disco Time	III	10	19
Right on Time and Ready to Go	III	12	19
Walking Dotty	IV	2	21
One Step Ahead	IV	4	22
Lifting Weights	IV	5	22
Triplet Squats	V	1	27
Groovy Dance	V	2	27
Street Dance	V	5	28
Stumble, Trip	V	7	30
Tiptoes	V	8	30

SIMPLE TRIPLE METER

TITLE	*Grp.*	*No.*	*Page*
Waltzing on Stilts	III	1	15
Tiptoe, Don't Get Caught	III	2	15
A Bit Stop-Start	III	3	15
Working the Punchbag	III	8	18
Gentle Skip	III	11	19
Tied Together for a Mountain Walk	IV	1	21
Stretch It Out	IV	3	21
Awkward Dancing	IV	6	22
Wobbly Piggyback	V	3	27
At a Canter	V	6	28
Keepie-Uppies	V	10	31

SIMPLE DUPLE METER

TITLE	*Grp.*	*No.*	*Page*
March on the Spot	III	4	16
Stepping in Time	III	5	16
Baby Steps	III	6	16
Gym Beats	V	4	28
Right on Time and Ready to Go	V	12	31

COMPOUND METERS

TITLE	*Grp.*	*No.*	*Page*
1-and-a, 2-and-Away We Go!	IV	7	24
Wriggling Toes	IV	8	24
Twirling on Toes	IV	9	24
Graceful Swinging	IV	10	25
A Hop and a Skip	IV	11	25
Right on Time and Ready to Go	IV	12	25
On the Water	V	9	30
Down the Rope, Inch by Inch	V	11	31

A DOZEN A DAY

Available Online and from All Good Music Stores

Mini Book: HL00404073

Preparatory Book: HL00414222

Book 1: HL00413366

Book 2: HL00413826

Book 3: HL00414136

Book 4: HL00415686

Anthology: HL00158307

Exclusively Distributed By
HAL•LEONARD®
A Muse Group Company